So Many Words,
An Anthology
By Arra Lindemann

Arra Lindemann has asserted her right to be identified as the author of this book. All rights reserved. No part of this publication may be reproduced, stored in a retrieval system, or transmitted, in any form or by any means, electronic, mechanical, photocopying, recording or otherwise, without the prior permission of the author.

Acknowledgements:

This second anthology of poetry could not have been written without the following people:

Combichrist: Thanks for making my first concert an awesome night, I dedicate this book to you in thanks.

Emigrate: This studio Project has inspired my work in many ways, some of these poems would not have been written otherwise.

Rammstein: Dankeschön Till, Richard, Christoph, Ollie, Paul und Flake. Diese Gedichte sind für euch alle.

Darren Shan: Thanks for your continued support, without you I couldn't have published one book let alone a second.

I would also like to thank my publishers; they have turned my life around by publishing my books.

To my beloved Dark Stars and to everybody who has helped me on this long road I want to thank you all from deep down inside my heart.

Lastly I would like to thank everybody who has purchased my books. I appreciate your support.

Contents:

Section 1: Poems About the Universe

Eclipse

The Planet

Darkness

Skyfire

The Stars

Fallen

Section 2: Political Poems

Fear

Silenced

Welcoming

Puppetry

Section 3: Observational Poems

Foxes and the Realities of Hunting

Changes

Look

Reality

Carers

Mannequins

Prisoners

Travelling

The City

Publicity

Section 4: Dark/Emotional Poems

The Truth About Abuse

A Pet's Goodbye

Depression

Dark Times

Shell

Feelings

Knife

Falling

Forgetting

Section 5: Poems About Sex

Sex-Simplified

Mining For Pearls

A Watery Metaphor

Fire and the Body

The Flames of Love

Love's Burning Fire

Chemical Reactions

Electrical Energy

Hunted

Body

Tree

Section 6: Poems About Nature, History and Animals

In The Spring

Quiet Nights

Summer Days

Rats

Remnants

Section 7: Poems About People

Normal

The Dark

Shallow

Humanity

Bring Me Down

Sacrifices

Acceptance

Passing On

Enigma

Return

Portrait

Rise

Section 8: Metaphorical Poems

The Phoenix

I am

Vampires

Lost

Section 9: Miscellaneous Poems

The Curse of Life

Science and the World

Waiting

Wishes

A Lack of Inspiration

Chains

Doors

Chaos

Section 1: Poems About the Universe

Eclipse:

The sun will rise and set many times in my life, thick grey clouds cover the rays of light in a vapoury veil of night,

The jealous moon must wait for the Sun to fade, the sky will then exchange the sunset for starlight as the Earth swaps its position again,

My dawn is your nightfall and your evening is my morning, I awake to a new day whilst you are asleep and snoring,

The moon envies the sunshine for It knows that it will never be as bright, secretly the sun cries for it wants to see how the stars form patterns in the sky,

Eventually they both meet while the Earth acts as a go between, for a few moments the moon can be happy as it transforms the daytime into night and shines solely,

This brief eclipse is a deal that's been struck with the sun and moon so that both can experience each other's abilities, the Earth makes them take turns and it helps to keep things balancing nicely.

The Planet:

If the Earth is a body then it is most definitely alive, the wind is like its whispering voice and the stars are its eyes,

When the Earth is annoyed it erupts in a fiery volcanic anger, when the Earth is sad it cries so much that it floods,

The planet bares so many scars which will never be completely healed, we don't always notice them but they are very real,

The Earth is our mother and it gives us life, if people continue to walk along this destructive path then the planet will die and this is what you must realise,

The land is the Earth's skin and it cannot be owned by anybody, cutting into it will make it bleed soil and stones which everyone can see,

The world is alive and it provides everything we need to survive, when you walk upon its skin and drink its tears remember that without Mother Earth we wouldn't be here,

Give thanks to the planet for your life whilst there is still time, for our home is slowly being ruined and I've already seen some ominous signs,

Please change your ways before it's too late, if persons choose not to do this then it'll be the end of the human race and that doesn't sound too great.

Darkness

The night falls but the moon isn't visible, however one thousand or more stars glitter like crystals,

The sun shines even when there are clouds in the sky, it is also a star and it glows from afar.

*Skyfire:

The sky is alight and the sunset is ablaze with flames, for they burn through the blue and the whole place glows with an orange hue,

Sun rays reflect upon the sea as if they were laser beams, the water burns on the surface but underneath it is cold enough to freeze,

Skyfire in its entirety has filled up the horizon completely, there is no longer a deep greyish sea but a body of water that is coloured unusually,

Nothing is ever what it seems and how the planet functions is a mystery, for it isn't controlled by anybody but that's not necessarily a bad thing,

Skyfire ignites this world and the only way to put it out is to cover it with night's blanket, the stars act as embers and they remain lit even when an overlay of cloud hides everything.

*Skyfire is a word which I have invented for the purposes of this poem, it is not in any dictionary and the definition of the word is: A time when the sunset gives the sky a fiery deep orange/yellow colour which looks like a blaze, that is Skyfire.

The Stars:

Look up to the skies because stars become visible at night, for they make up many constellations which have been studied by humans over time,

Our ancestors saw the same stars that we can see except they named them differently, for every country has astrological stories embedded in its history,

Some may see a maiden and others notice a bear, it depends upon the time of year as to what stars are in view and where,

They may only be made from burning gas but stars never seem to fade, our nearest one is the sun and it is more than a million miles away.

Fallen:

Fallen stars descend so far and they shoot across the sky, a flash of light brightens up the night but only for a brief moment of time.

Section 2: Political Poems

Fear:

These moments of fear seem to be forever drawing near, however the Soldiers have the strength to fight because they must do what's right,

We stand side by side not knowing if we will live or die, when they drop bombs on us we fire rockets over their heads which light up the skies,

Many run as they fear for their lives and nobody wants to be posted on the front lines, for these people have been left with nothing more than memories of better times,

It almost seems like the country's leaders haven't got a clue how to settle this dispute, the continuous violence has left many civilians without shelter or food,

We must make a stand against those who commit atrocities on our land, for it is our blood which now stains the once golden sand,

Help us to rebuild our towns and cities because we cannot continue to live like this, the aid workers need to step in and attend to those who are sick,

Fear is what refugees have to face every single day, you can see it in their child's eyes as they stand still and do nothing but shake,

The people deserve better than this and it's no surprise that they want out of their country's dictatorship,

The government must change its policies and become a democracy, that's the only way to proceed if they wish to end the war and save what's left of their country.

Silenced:

On a silent night nobody arrives to rescue them from this plight, no screams come from their tongues when heads have been with a knife sliced,

Blood drips from the stump that was once their neck, now hear a thud as this dead body hits the deck,

Silent are those who are guilty because if they cannot speak then what hope is there for an innocent like me?

We run and flee to a place of safety but the border men say that we cannot pass into the country, take my children at least I cry but all they do is turn a blind eye,

Help us finally be free from the tyranny but nobody cares about a woman like me, the government won't even give out water that's clean so all of us are thirsty after our risky journey,

To stay silent should be a crime and no human should have to die when the people in charge can't get it right,

Please hear us now as our weakened footsteps touch the ground and the port comes into sight, we are all tired and suffering after walking so many miles,

Give us a chance to live with you in peace for we have not all been convicted of atrocities, most of us are young mothers or elderly and all we ask is to be treated humanely,

How much more innocent blood has to flow down the roads and onto the streets? Can you not hear our panicking heartbeats?

We are Syrians and you are our sanctuary, please save us from the bombs that are being dropped daily,

I hope that we can all get along peacefully in one multicultural society, at least that's what I want for my family.

Welcoming:

Welcome to the utopia that I call Earth, for this planet has been providing me with everything I need to live since the day of my birth,

Some countries live in harmony whilst others are forced to survive In a dystopian society,

Government ministers have made plenty of mistakes in their time, they stand idly by whilst their citizens suffer and die; this clearly isn't right,

People are forced to flee as refugees, they cross several territories whilst seeking a place where their children can live in peace,

Welcoming so many people even in an emergency puts a strain on everybody, resources are limited so use them wisely,

Help those who need it the most and send the others to another place that they can call home, this way we'll keep our borders secure but not totally closed.

Puppetry:

If the brain is a box which is full of thoughts then somebody with a key needs to open the lock and let these feelings out,

People need to learn how to express themselves and speak the words which are on their minds out loud,

We aren't puppets and we have no need for super marianation which controls our every move, like it or not this is the truth,

Don't let the injustices of this world continue, everybody is equal and if you don't act now then someone else will have to,

The government are puppeteers and they love to put on a show, however we can keep the stage curtains closed by simply telling them no,

The performance being referred to is an election and government leaders think that they can pull the strings, in reality we're the masters of puppetry and we know how much damage a vote of no confidence can bring.

Section 3: Observational Poems

Foxes and the Realities of Hunting:

Foxes are tracked down by a pack of hounds because farmers say that they kill lambs, this is just an excuse to take part in barbaric activities which need to be completely banned,

If the hounds catch a fox they rip it to shreds, the only mercy the fox gets is a bullet through the head,

Foxes are dug out from their earth and chased down country lanes, they run across fields hoping to escape from the dogs on their trail but not every fox gets away,

I think that it's time for humans to change their ways, people should protect wildlife rather than killing it for a thrill just to keep their lust for blood at bay,

If you have absolutely no money then hunt to eat by all means but don't do it frequently, take only what you need to survive and let the rest of the world's creatures Live peacefully.

Changes:

Over time many things change, each passing day creates both natural and artificial alterations to the planet which take place in some way,

What once was a green field is now a playground, for a barn has been converted into a house and trees will be cut down to build a relief road leading to the town,

Acres of land are levelled out and turned into building sites, for the human population is exploding at an alarming rate and this doesn't seem right,

Changes happen all the time and some are necessary but others are just caused by people and their greed, for they have a desire to make money above everything,

Wake up and smell the coffee; if humans continue to live like this then the world will end up in very bad shape, there are people suffering needlessly but things can still change for the better hopefully,

I wish that people would change their attitudes but it isn't likely, for money makes the world go round and that is the problem with modern society.

Look:

Look around at the world for there isn't really a man sitting on a cloud controlling everything, the only person in charge is yourself and you can pick your own destiny,

Look at the trees and flowers which give the Earth its beauty, feel free to bite an apple which is green and juicy but remember to admire the planet for growing such treats,

Look at the water, the waves and life under the sea, dive down deep to experience the ocean with its salty wealth of fish and the stunning coral reef,

Look at the mountains and their snowy peaks, notice how the mist swirls around them like a veil of mystery which hasn't yet been breached by humanity,

Look at how everything is in harmony whilst hearing many different birds sing, watch the sun setting as stars become visible to the naked eye,

People must learn to appreciate these simple things or they'll never know what the Earth can provide,

Following a natural life is for those people who can live off the land in order to survive, for in doing so they have no need of technology which has become a part of modern times.

Reality:

I'm sitting here silently looking at the trees and mountains which seem to be eternally green, for this place is full of more purity and beauty than I've ever seen,

There is frailty around me as the natural order of things comes into play, the hillside must make way for all the things that men will want to create,

Houses have now been built from the trees which used to stand so gracefully, what once was undisturbed woodland is now home to many factories,

The objects which these places produce get sold commercially to make money for the ever-expanding community,

This is the sad reality of living in the twenty first century, unfortunately this planet is suffering because of a desire to build things upon it which are completely unnecessary.

Carers:

Carers are meant to help those who have daily needs but this doesn't happen necessarily,

Carers drive around to lots of houses cooking and cleaning for people who can't manage for themselves, carers do everything Including fetching things from high shelves,

Carers get paid a pittance for the work that they do, they get home late and their schedule won't change even when they get abused,

Some carers take advantage of those who are vulnerable, these are the bad eggs and they belong in jail,

I believe that most carers are angels in disguise, they're the good people who help the ill and disabled live independent lives.

Mannequins:

Mannequins stand behind a wall of glass and each one is adorned in a different style, they've got no heart or mind and they're devoid of life in their soulless eyes,

Moulded into shape from melted plastics and then put out on display, these mannequins are moved to different locations every day,

Outfits are modelled on their cold hard bodies and they're nearly always posed, sometimes they aren't even fully clothed,

No breath or life comes from inside and there is no warmth or flesh, they just appear in shop windows wearing whatever fashion says should be advertised next.

Prisoners:

If you think that prisoners have got it easy then you're wrong, for they're under lock and key and that's where they belong,

Prisoners wake up in a cell and every day is the same routine, they walk around the exercise yard before a privileged few get to watch TV,

A weekly visit from family for prisoners who are lucky, the rest are on lock down for public safety,

Prisoners have a horrible time but that's the price to pay if they commit crimes, some criminals die inside which serves them right for taking another person's life,

Think of the victims too and the suffering that they go through, for the innocent must be given justice and that's what the legal system is designed to do.

Travelling:

I'm going to the station and getting on the train, it's going to take me away to a brand-new place,

People read their papers as they try to kill some time, I would do the same as them but I left my book behind,

Nobody can foresee their future journeys, they wake up in a village and they go to sleep in a city,

Planes, buses and trains are the main forms of transport, most people drive cars but some prefer to ride a horse,

Travelling around the world is what I'm aiming to do, for I wish to experience different things and try lots of new food.

The City:

If the city is a heart which beats daily then surely it means that the surrounding land is its body,

We feel energy from these cities which never sleep, buildings are taller than trees and every street offers business opportunities,

Lost in a stream of lights so bright they're damaging my eyes, there's no quiet place to rest at night for the city is awake and very much alive,

I'll watch the sunrise from on top of a housing block that's high-rise, there are lots of building sites so industrial machinery looks like a natural part of the skyline,

People live in synergy and to them this city is the place to be, personally it is the countryside that brings to me a feeling of security,

I like nothing better than having grass under my feet instead of pavements and concrete, after all big cities don't do anything for me.

Publicity:

I'm in the papers again today which is the price you pay for fame, every photo the Paparazzi sell makes money and they see it as just another game,

This is called publicity and I don't mind being interviewed on the TV, however I still want to take part in regular activities,

My life is surrounded by flashes of light all the time, I can't even walk down the street without someone asking if they can get a selfie or something signed,

I honestly do not mind this lifestyle and it's great when I haven't got to stand in line for events, I use the side entrance and then sneak out the back when the after show ends,

This is modern celebrity life and people want fame but they never seem to understand what it is actually like,

It is not easy and money doesn't always come instantly,

Set a good example to your fans and be happy, that's the only advice I can give really.

Section 4: Dark/Emotional Poems

The Truth About Abuse:

Like a moth drawn to flames I was sucked in, my innocence was lost via blood and pain and that's the secret I hide within,

I could neither speak nor scream whilst this was happening to me, he held a knife to my throat before stealing my purity,

I stayed silent for too long so my rapist walks the streets instead of being in jail where he belongs,

I urge people to speak out against things like this, you don't have to suffer in silence like I did,

One bruise is too many and don't listen to any of his excuses, he'll beg for forgiveness but don't ever give it to him,

Abusers don't deserve to be forgiven and their actions won't be forgotten either,

Don't allow yourself to become a victim, fight back because he won't expect it,

He thinks you're weak without him but he's nothing without you and that's the truth.

A Pet's Goodbye:

Now that I'm curling up to sleep I say to you please don't weep, for you have taken very good care of me and that is plain to see,

When I shall cross the rainbow bridge note that it is you who I will miss, parting is hard to do I know but in the end we all must go, this goodbye message I send because I have been laid to rest,

I have entered into an eternal sleep but a piece of your heart I will keep, please save another and let them have my place, so that in time they will fill up your empty space.

Depression:

These dark days have broken my heart, my love of things will now depart,

A blackness exists inside my mind, I try to cover it up with a smile but still it rears its head from time to time,

Depression is like a shadow that won't leave me alone, it creeps up from behind thereby ruining my daily life,

There may not be any signs of Illness but depression is a very real thing, people tell you to "Snap out of it" but trust me it's not that easy.

Dark Times:

People are struggling to make ends meet because the cost of living rises frequently, bills must be paid but there's never enough money to cover everything,

These are dark times even though it is the twenty first century, we have technology but not what we necessarily need,

Different countries are fighting endlessly, once thriving cities are now piles of dust and rubble because the bombings will not cease,

Dark times are these when children don't get enough to eat, they get left alone to beg on the streets,

Dark times come when young men walk around with guns and shoot stuff for fun, the real trouble starts when they start dealing drugs,

Throughout these dark times the strong individuals survive, it is the rest who are fighting to stay alive.

Shell:

I feel as though I could cry but no tears will come from these eyes, I cannot even describe what I'm feeling on the inside,

So many things are playing on my mind and this happens all the time, I need to clear my head and start thinking straight for once in my life,

I am a shell of my former self but nobody can tell because I've learnt to shield my emotions well, my heart feels heavy and as such its weighing my soul down,

I've been calling out for help but my voice seems to have failed me, now I tend to sit alone and think about things quietly.

Feelings:

Nobody hears or sees the silent tears which are rolling down my face, I feel so lost but I cannot go back to that place,

How could one guy make me cry so many times? I missed the signs and now I realise that this relationship just wasn't going right,

Being reminded of his name brings me nothing but bad feelings and pain, I hope to never hear from him again,

I wonder if this wound will ever heal for sadness is what I feel, my heart was ripped from my chest so these emotions are both raw and real,

I wish my feelings would fade away or at least change rather than always staying the same,

I wish for the day when I'll be happy again, however it'll take some time to recover from this heartbreak,

I split with my fiancé because he was a cheat and he didn't know the meaning of the word loyalty,

As a result of his actions we're no longer engaged and at the end of the day marriage is just a piece of paper anyway.

Knife:

I hold in my hands a knife and its deadly bloodstained blade shines in the light, for some knives are just a tool but in the wrong hands they can be lethal,

Cold hard steel encased in a sheath of human skin as the tip is pushed deeper in, this metal implement has just claimed another victim,

Dark are the nights when people walk the streets carrying knives for they are used in many crimes, self-defence is one thing but nobody has the right to take a life,

How many more young people will die because of knives or by being in the wrong place at the wrong time?

Now is our chance to take a stand by cleaning up the streets and making the cities safe for everybody, otherwise young innocent blood will continue to be spilt unnecessarily.

Falling:

I'm sliding down the slippery slope called life as if it were a roller-coaster ride, for I have realised that the further I fall will increase the distance that I must climb before my mistakes can be rectified,

I sometimes feel like I'm falling down into a bleak place, for I have had dark thoughts running through my brain and I wish that they would just go away,

I try to ignore the negativity that seems to be surrounding me, what has happened to the positive energy? It's almost as though it has been sucked out of me,

I believe that everybody needs a safety net occasionally or you would fall indefinitely, after all humans don't have wings and having the ability to grow them in an emergency isn't very likely.

Forgetting:

I want to forget everything you've put me through, I know that I'm not perfect but then again neither are you,

Drug dealing scum is what you are and prison is where you belong, after all you've sold coke to fifteen year olds and that's beyond wrong,

If you think I'm crazy then take a good look at yourself, after all I'm not the one who used drugs and then suffered from a major come-down,

You're dead as far as I'm aware and forgetting you was easy, I deserve better than this and I don't want your negative energy around me.

Section 5: Poems About Sex

Sex-Simplified:

So many sperm seem to be released into a woman's body, they swim towards the egg cell which has come directly from the ovaries,

A woman is a vessel that is made from flesh and bone, can you hear the sexual almost orgasmic moans? She will scream in sheer ecstasy when deep inside her the guys' manhood is buried,

This is sex at its best and exactly how it's supposed to be, listen to her heart pounding as it seems to skip a few beats,

How she breathes so erratically is no mystery, it is to do with sexual stimulation building up inside her body,

As great as sex can be remember to have fun responsibly, make sure to protect yourself against unwanted pregnancy and sexually transmitted disease or you could end up very sick indeed.

Mining for Pearls:

If a thin pane of glass acting as a door must be with a hammer smashed then it will surely crack,

There is no longer a barrier in-between to prevent this from happening, for the entrance has been well and truly breached,

The piston full of fluid goes back and forth, it's trying to flood the inner tunnels because that's what it's been designed for,

The jewel minor is searching for pearls as they are symbols of purity, they hang upon strings like a chandelier but they cannot be reached easily,

A pearl will occasionally drop from Its string and when this happens it gets discarded, single pearls without strings will split and divide several times if they're not protected carefully,

The jewel minor should be happy if he finds what he seeks because he enters the tunnel every week,

He leaves behind a trace of himself each time so that he can stake his claim when its required,

If a pearl grows too big then it must be pulled through the tunnel exit, the team mustn't cause any damage to it because a fully sized pearl would be very expensive to fix.

A Watery Metaphor:

From the moment of conception water gives us life, we started off as a primordial soup and now we're floating around in a fluid sack without which we couldn't survive,

We start off as a single cell which divides, after nine months we come down the birth canal which expands and contracts over a few hours so that we can begin our life,

If semen runs like a river then every sperm becomes a ship and the egg is a dock, if you close the gates then you will be safe so always use a condom,

Ejaculation is like a giant wave crashing against the shore, I just hope that people understand this watery metaphor,

If two people can set sail and reach the island of paradise then they'll have a good time, the waters are usually calm but when a storm comes in the ship is likely to be capsized,

Whether a couple sinks or survives is for them to decide, they have the helm in their hands and only they can choose how to sail their way through life.

Fire and the Body:

There is fire inside the mind but it's hard to describe for these are flames of desire,

Within the heart and soul burns a constant blaze of emotions, hormones are the embers which spark and set bodies on fire,

Passion is an inferno which no amount of water will dowse, for lust is the fuel which these arsonists have at their disposal.

The Flames of Love:

If love is like a fire then it burns deep inside our hearts, for passion Is the fuel which ignites these flames from the very start,

These cinders of wantonness take hold of our minds, what begins as an ember becomes a fiery blaze of emotions over time,

Love is a power that cannot be controlled, it's a force which is felt by both young and old,

To be in love is to suffer from a disease because people don't act rationally; they become zombies who only think about lustful things,

When the flames of love are lit a tiny spark is all it takes to set our bodies on fire, for we become an inferno that is energised with scorching desires.

Love's Burning Fire:

Love sets my heart on fire and its embers glow eternally with desire, my soul has been ignited by this flame,

My body is a vessel that carries the fuel and that fuel is passion, it makes you crave moments of time when all you can feel is heat and ecstasy as these fuels mix and bind,

Love makes you blind and you can feel nothing but the scorching temperatures inside, there is no escape and no amount of water will dowse these flames that cannot die,

We lay in wait for somebody to consume us with their fiery embrace, for this is where bodies and souls become as one in a spiritual way,

We listen to what our hearts are saying inside rather than hearing the little voice in our mind that gives us sound advice,

Hearts are like sponges for they absorb both love and pain but human hearts can also break, please remember that there is much at stake no matter which paths in life you choose to take.

Chemical Reactions:

Like sugar and sulphur love can be either sweet or bitter, for chemical reactions make our bodies change so that men and women will never be the same,

Emotions and hormones both play their part, our brains release them in different quantities and that is a fine balancing art,

Sex is like a drug for not only is it addictive but certain humans never seem to get enough of it,

Having sex regularly is healthy but sleeping with too many different people risks both unwanted pregnancy and disease,

Like it or not life is an experiment and we have to learn which things mix, however some of our natural human urges may just push us to the brink.

Electrical Energy:

The passion and hormones in my body are flowing through me like a machine that's full of electricity,

These sensations are everywhere and I can feel them tingling, they're building up within me,

A bed is like a battery, if two bodies combined make a circuit then they will conduct sexual energy,

One kiss can flip the switch making the circuit complete because there are so many feelings pulsing through my body, it is as if carnal desires and electricity are exactly the same thing.

Hunted:

You are a hunter and there is no escape for I know that must be claimed, I am prey which should be chased because I am fair game,

Pursue me, seduce me, make me yours and in exchange I will show you exactly why I'm worth hunting for,

I can neither run nor hide, just one look into the hunter's eyes and I am hypnotised,

I go to bed with him knowing that he will be good to me, he is a master of his craft and he will set me free,

One kiss from him is like lightning and fire combined, such energy and power cannot be described,

His voice is alluring and he encourages me, it doesn't hurt even though he is buried deep inside of my body,

I feel this hunger and it's like every inch of me is burning from within, I am yearning for the hunter to touch my skin,

If I were a dove my white feathers would now be stained with blood because a few drops have come from me, for you have claimed your prize and I am now a trophy,

Bodily fluids mix with mine and we enter into a realm of paradise, it's like sheer ecstasy and it feels divine,

I see stars in his eyes and oh how they shine so bright, I love him in a way that I cannot define,

I know that this hunter will give me many a sleepless night, However I do not mind as long as he treats me right.

Body:

Warm body, hot breath, soft to the touch and enticingly wet, passionate love with burning desires, it's time to ignite your inner fire,

Lips brushing against skin, moaning, pleading, but being gentle so as not to cause any bleeding,

In your eyes she can see your hunger for her, her body joins to yours and then you will feel the lust within,

Exchanging fluids and fighting for control, you continue pulsing deeply until she screams in ecstasy repeatedly,

Head rush, adrenaline pumping, craving more so that the sensations don't end,

Playing with each other, teasing and licking, this makes it feel even better,

You and her lying on the bed hoping that you can continue to explore each other, sex is a way to extend pleasure but remember to give and receive in equal measure.

Trees:

Some men can be compared to trees because they stand taller than other human beings, so I begin to ask myself how strong are they exactly?

A man's heart is like a giant kernel for it grows love and it is cared for by many, his soul is like a leaf because it is always evergreen and it will live on eternally,

He has many roots which join him up with his family for these little sprouts will grow and expand continuously, his energy flows through each and every twig so that they all remain connected,

From every man comes a few thousand seeds but only one or two may germinate inside a woman's body, please plant your pips carefully or you'll end up with little saplings and you know exactly what I mean.

Section 6: Poems About Nature, History and Animals

In Spring:

In the Spring the bird sings, the trees are green and children play in the sunlight,

In the Spring there is colour-play in the garden with the flowers, they are beautiful and delicate.

Quiet Nights:

Late at night owls make their silent flight, through the woodland and between the trees they glide whilst the moon is in the sky,

To human ears it is a peaceful time but after sunset the forest comes alive, nocturnal creatures come out to play because they sleep during the day,

Rabbits run from sight as they're chased by a blur of red and white, it is the vixen and she must hunt or her cubs won't eat anything tonight,

Even on these quiet nights things are happening all the time, it's how nature has been designed and those who are lucky get to witness it with their own eyes.

Summer Days:

Sunlight shines upon the hillside and a flock of sheep are bleating, these warm days bring clear blue skies and birds can be seen perching in the trees,

On summer days people lay on the beach with not a care in the world, they lie there for hours on end until their skin turns to raspberry red,

This is the time of year when the teachers give a cheer, with no more lessons until September they can enjoy a night out on the town and drink a few beers,

Summer is coming here but unfortunately it cannot stay, for nature has decided that the winter must have a say and therefore take its place,

Make the most of these summer nights with cloudless skies and stars glittering bright, for the full moon provides a glowing beacon of light,

Summertime is when dozens of rabbits hop around the fields, however most farmers will turn crop eating bunnies into healthy meals.

Rats:

Eyes glinting in the darkness, whiskers twitching like electrical wires, teeth sharper than a knife and a coat of brown velvet,

Silently going from room to room, between the walls and under the floorboards, this is where rats reign and here you'll find their pink, newly born spawn,

Breeding, squeaking, gnawing and scurrying around hoping that they won't be found, rats can live anywhere be it in a house or in town,

Please don't use these animals in lab tests or other experimental projects, for rats can be taught to detect land mines and in doing so they've earnt respect by saving people's lives.

Remnants:

Under the soil are the rusty remnants of what was once a fighter plane, the only thing left now is an empty metal shell that's seen better days and the guns which have been discovered won't be fired again,

The tip of a broken wing, a smashed windscreen with many pieces and the blades are becoming visible as the soil is brushed away, this is a big find for those who are interested in our history,

It is not every day that you locate a missing Spitfire that was shot down in 1943, the past is being revealed slowly by the archaeological team but they always seem to need more funding,

A skeleton comes out of the ground bone by bone, the skull is cracked like an egg and the pilot's name remains unknown,

So many brave young men gave up their lives between 1939 and 1945 and that happened on both sides, the people that survived this awful time should never forget those who made the ultimate sacrifice.

Section 7: Poems About People

Normal:

Being normal is so boring but it is deemed to be acceptable, however the question on my mind remains the same: what is normal anyway?

Society decides what normality is and they like to put people in boxes, if you don't fit into a certain place then you get treated differently to the rest of humanity,

Normality means getting up and going to work every day, if you don't work then you can't pay your way,

What if you're disabled? Are you abnormal for losing a leg in battle?

What if you can't hear or see properly but you're still able bodied? Does this make you less normal than the rest of the people?

Gay, bi and transgender people have only recently gained marriage equality in this country,

They can't help being different biologically yet they're still shunned in some communities,

Normality is what society says the majority should be, if you're in a minority group then that's OK with me,

At the end of the day we're human beings and nature has made all of us unique for a reason.

The Dark:

Step into night's eternal embrace and prevent the light from entering this place,

We wear shadows as if they were cloaks for they hold the darkness within, we've got black hearts and even blacker souls but that's just the beginning,

Come and dance in the moonbeams, let them set you free from a world of conformity,

This is our time and we welcome the creatures of light to experience our lives, we mean you no harm unless you do something that we do not like,

Goths aren't evil; we don't drink blood or perform Satanic spells either, stereotyping gives us a bad name and the bullying we get makes us afraid,

We don't want any trouble and we do our best to live in peace with our communities, in fact we're big softies in reality,

We welcome you to join us in celebrating because it is World Goth Day, have fun by all means but remember to stay safe.

Shallow:

Some people are so shallow that they only think about designer clothing, their image is more important to them than helping those in need,

Some humans are so self-absorbed, they like you if you're rich but they ignore you if you're poor,

Some people think upon what they can gain but not what they can give, they pay no attention to the people who are suffering,

The human race needs to change its ways as we can't go on like this, for too many people are living in poverty without the most basic necessities,

The shallowness of people is what makes me angry, for they look down their noses at everybody who isn't in their clique,

Not everybody is born wealthy in fact the majority are born into humble families, some people will earn a lot of money and others will never make ends meet,

My point is that people should be treated with compassion and decency whether or not they have money,

Money makes people shallow and greedy because they'll always want more, for endless possibilities await and having disposable cash is the key to opening the doors.

Humanity:

If you ripped open my skin you'd reveal flesh and bones, my body parts would be exposed and humanity is what they'd show,

I am not a trophy to be won because I am a living being, I just want to be treated respectfully like every person should be,

None of us are perfect because it's our flaws which make us unique, without them we'd lose our individuality and we would end up like cloned copies,

Nature made us this way so that nobody would ever look the same, we're one of a kind at the end of the day and I think that's great.

Bring Me Down:

I've got fire in my soul and I'm tired of being told, you've never made my life that easy, I have water in my brain and my mind's flooded with words again but that's called poetry,

With lightning in my heart I don't know where to start and the night's drawing in fast, I think I'll rest my head but that's not what my mind says and I'm left wondering how long this insomnia will last,

Nobody shall ever bring me down because I have too much to lose, I've been working hard all this time and I too have suffered from abuse,

All my life I've had nothing but now I have something, I have a dream that I wish to achieve so I'm filled with positive energy and the determination to succeed,

You'll try to bring me down and I am aware of the rumours that are going around the town, I have proof that what I say is the truth so Just let it go now,

If you wish to bring me down then go ahead and try, you won't get anywhere near me because of my security, I don't like having guards but at least now I can go outside without being in fear of my life.

Sacrifices:

During our lifetime all of us will make at least one sacrifice for the benefit Of somebody, this could mean selling your possessions to raise money for a family who have nothing,

It is never easy when you live in poverty but that is why we have charities, these are special organisations which can help those who are in need,

They ask for donations and volunteers to aid them so that their projects will be finished and complete, they aim to assist as many as they can but a lack of supplies mean that not everybody will be reached,

Making a sacrifice to help Somebody else is a very brave thing to do, some may choose to give out food whilst others give up their free time and put it to good use,

Sometimes people will sacrifice their own lives in order for others to survive, these are the heroes that I recognise and they deserve to be remembered long after they die.

Acceptance:

Acceptance is to respect a person's lifestyle, how they choose to live shouldn't matter as long as it makes them smile,

What gives us the right to judge others? Can't we all just mutually respect one another?

Haters are going to hate, at the end of the day I don't really care what you've got to say,

I won't allow anybody to stand in the way of me achieving my aims, people need to stop playing their ridiculous mind games,

I was used as a scapegoat and I've said this from the start, in truth I'm a good person with a pure heart,

I've closed the door on my mistakes and I'm focusing upon what the future has in store, I ask only to be accepted despite my many flaws.

Passing On:

Just because you cannot see me it doesn't mean that I am not there, for I'm the whisper in the wind and the warmth in the summer air,

Passing on is sad and many people cry, however we aren't immortal and we will eventually die,

Death can finally set us free from pain as our physical bodies change, flesh begins to rot away and bones become nothing more than skeletal remains,

Despite what others may think or say I believe that human souls go onto a peaceful resting place,

It has to be done this way or the Earth would run out of space, it may sound upsetting but it's true for every living race.

Enigma:

To me he is an enigma wrapped around a mystery. Who is this man that I look at so admiringly? What does he do? How does he live and to which charities does he give?

Where does he reside to enjoy his day to day life? Is he married with a child and a wife? I have so many questions in my head but so little time,

Does this man know that I exist? Will we ever pass each other on the street? Would he even recognise me? I shall have to wait patiently for an opportunity when we're able to meet and speak to one another briefly,

I think all he wants sometimes is to live his life away from the public eye, it's horrible when journalists are in his face or trying to climb over the electrified gates,

He rests in a tent at night because of the peace and solitude he finds, for camping enables him to sleep under the stars in the sky without any worries going through his mind.

Return:

A gaping space that was empty Until recently has been filled in and this makes me complete, for it's hard to be separated from a member of my family,

My brother was born one way however he's changed because he now thinks of himself as female, the love I have for my new sister remains the same regardless of how she spends her days,

We shall balance each other out like yin and yang, for I am the light in her dark mind and she provides me with shade on the path of life when it becomes too bright,

The missing piece of my broken heart has been returned to me, for we both bare scars from our ordeal and now the cracks need time to heal.

Portrait:

If life is a portrait then the best moments should be framed, each memory becomes a photograph that gets placed in an album inside our brains,

Life is hard make no mistake but looking back upon the highlights is sometimes all it takes to put a smile on your face,

Snapshots of life become frozen in time, even after many years have gone by you can look at an old photo and remember where you were on that night,

Capture as much as you can on film or you could make models from clay, that way the people of the future can see how we chose to live out our days,

Maybe in the future your family portrait will be hung up in a gallery, then people can see where their ancestors came from originally,

Let's all try to go down in history by achieving many good things and living out our dreams, when our bones are found buried in the ground we will become part of an archaeological study and that's fine by me.

Rise:

Now is the time to rise and rebel against this mundane life, every day it's the same routine: get up, get dressed, go to work, pay your bills and feed the family or that is what it's supposed to be but I say it's time to set yourselves free from this monotony,

Rebel against the norm, go to work without the correct uniform, make mistakes and let someone else take the blame, drink yourself into a paralytic state and stay up late,

Sleep with who you like, snort coke up your nose and then party all night, dance and sing like it means nothing, explore the four corners of the world and lie under the starry skies,

What I mean is that you'll never get anywhere in life if you sit at a desk and answer phones all the time, it's fine to go out occasionally and get buck wild after all everybody has a rebellious side that's just waiting to come alive.

Section 8: Metaphorical Poems

The Phoenix:

In a blazing burst of flames the phoenix is born, she is not of this world but still she comes forth,

Flames come in waves as she flies through the sky, for she leaves behind a trail of light that makes Paradise look like it's on fire,

The phoenix is a creature from the Greek myths and she doesn't actually exist, however she is a metaphor for rebirth and I find that quite poetic,

The phoenix dies in an inferno as she spontaneously combusts before your eyes, however she shall arise from the pile of ashes in order to begin a new life,

In reality this applies to people who wish to leave their past behind, everybody deserves a second chance to get things right and no-one should have to run or hide whilst fearing for their lives.

I am:

I'm an angel with wings or I'm a bird who always sings, I am the Summer breeze and the gales which knock down trees,

I'm the midnight shadows and the moonbeams, I'm the one who is heard but never seen,

I'm the clouds in the sky and the tears in your eye, I'm the thunder and lightning that electrifies your life,

I'm the force behind the changing seasons, I'm the reason for the sunrise and the flowing tides,

I'm Mother Earth and I've protected the planet since its birth, I shall guard the animals and plants until the end of time as that's my appointed task.

Vampires:

Creatures of myth and legend are they who drink blood from a human's vein, when the clock strikes midnight the darkness hides them like a cloak and they melt away into the shadows,

When they feed they howl like wolves for the animal inside them comes alive, vampires are weak in the daylight so they sleep in coffins or crypts to avoid the sun's lethal rays until it is time for them to rise,

Blood flows so freely from a neck vein that it's like a stream and every drop gives life to these parasites, in truth you only see this happening in movies like Twilight,

I don't have much knowledge when it comes to dealing with people who suffer from split personalities, however an analogy of a vampire can be used as a metaphor to explain both sides of the human mind and how these people might feel,

The vampire also represents rebellion and a willingness to fight because everybody has a dark side but very rarely is it utilised, if you Can learn to balance both parts of who you are then you'll be fine.

Lost:

What now is lost cannot be regained for time ticks away and an hour cannot be replaced,

Minutes pass by as the sun makes the whole sky shine, the Earth turns partly towards the light whilst other places experience its dark side,

Losing grip on reality is like a disease that infects every inch of your mind and body, you have no sense of time and a week feels like an eternity,

I've lost the light inside because the voices of night keep calling my name, I feel the darkness embrace my soul as the moon waxes and wanes,

The girl you knew is lost and gone for I am not who I once was, all you shall hear is a mourning song as people file past my coffin one by one,

I've been reborn from sparking embers inside the cremation chamber and these roaring flames have enabled me to rise again,

You must realise that I'll never be quite the same and that's because every phoenix is unique in her own way.

Section 9: Miscellaneous Poems

The Curse of Life:

The curse of life is that one day you will die, however death can sometimes be a blessing in disguise,

Free from suffering and pain your body begins to degrade but your energy becomes part of the Earth again,

When it's your time you must leave family and friends behind, however kindred spirits will once again unite beyond the skies in Paradise,

This curse has existed since the beginning of time, what death takes away shall be replaced because that's the cycle of life.

Science and the World:

If this world was created then what has made it? If we evolved then where do we come from? Were we Indeed apes living in trees or have we always been a unique species?

There are many questions on a scientist's mind so they try to work out the most accurate answers before reporting what they find, some major discoveries have been made and because of this certain people have gained international recognition and fame,

One germ in a dish led to the manufacture of penicillin, experiments with radiation led to the detection of X Rays and thermometers were invented back in the eighteenth century,

As time passes the world changes; because of this we have adapted to a life surrounded by technology, many people owe their lives to science and medicines but education is the key to making new life saving machines,

Try to leave something behind that future generations can admire or remember you for, even if your contribution is tiny it's better than nothing and you only have one life So make the most of it by doing what makes you happy.

Waiting:

I'm waiting in the line which defines my life, I think to myself quietly if this will be the day that I finally shine,

Can I now stand under the spotlights? Will this be my time or should I just continue to hide?

I'm feeling nervous and I look far from perfect, however I smile and say that I'm alright or I'll never be prepared for these constant flashes of light,

This is my life but when I die I hope that I'll cross over to the other side, then I'll be floating high above the skies in Paradise,

For now though I am waiting to find out what my purpose in life is, after all there are many things that I am yet to experience.

Wishes:

I wish for happiness and to be loved for who I am, I hope to find my place in this world and be given the freedom to formulate a lifestyle plan,

I wish that people could look beyond my scarred face seeing as I've got a soul which always stays in the same place, I keep my heart locked away behind my ribcage where it's safe and then it shall not break,

I wish to choose my own fate and walk my own path through life as long as it remains straight, the occasional fork in the road is ok provided it doesn't lead me astray,

Last of all I wish for lots of good things come your way today and always, after all we are all members of the human race.

A Lack of Inspiration:

I'm suffering from a lack of inspiration and poetic words just won't come to me, you may as well put a padlock upon my mind and then throw away the key,

It's hard to concentrate when words pop into my head so randomly, I need to reorganise my literary thoughts and then set them free,

This lack of inspiration is driving me insane, I haven't written a poem for days and as a result my brain feels like it has been wrapped in chains,

I must seem so lazy but I can assure you that this isn't the case, for it takes time to rearrange the phrases inside my head space before posting them upon this page.

Chains:

Why are chains restricting me? I've gotta get loose and become free, break open this cage so that I can fly away and go across the sea,

Let me surf the waves and swim every day, humans aren't meant to be chained for we are not anybody's slaves,

Allow me to hunt and ride so that I can for myself provide, I wish explore the world and do my own thing for once in my life.

Doors:

To say that life is a room with many doors is not far from the truth however what lies behind these doors isn't always new, to recall one's life history is never easy but only by learning from the past can you decide upon your future,

When you walk through a door another one closes and some will never again be open to the same place, examine every option in order to succeed and seize every chance that comes your way,

Only by working hard can you achieve your dreams as nothing in life is free and nor should it be, one door slams shut in your face but another one unlocks nearby and this gives you necessary breathing space,

Be careful about which doors you choose to open; some will stay this way and others won't be what you hoped they would be, eventually you will find your key and that will lead to many opportunities,

Think things through and don't rush into anything because making a mistake now could cost you dearly, don't rely upon other people to turn your life around as you can do it for yourself,

Decide what you want from life but don't waste time on things which won't ever become reality, focus on positive things only and remember to expel all of your negativity.

Chaos:

Chaos reigns in the minds of those who are insane, they think about things which cannot be easily Explained,

Chaos is a crashing wave, chaos is an unrelenting storm of emotional pain, when chaos dominates nothing is safe,

Chaos is caused when random words pop into my head, they make no sense and when I can't put them into any form of order I tend to get stressed,

It is like having a mental dictionary which constantly updates, words stand out on every page and they fill my thoughts with a verbal maze,

I always seem to find my way through this strange place even when chaos comes out to play with my brain.